The Vessel of Truth

Maria Kitsios, LMT

Edited by Jaclyn Reuter
Cover Design by Danijela Mijailovic
Formatting by Tapioca Press

ISBN: 978-1-7378369-4-0 (paperback)
ISBN: 978-1-7378369-5-7 (ebook)

Publisher email address: mkitsios8@gmail.com

Printed by Maria Kitsios, in the United States of America.

First printing edition 2022

Dedicated to all the artists,
poets, musicians,
and expressive beings.
May you continue to inspire
through imagination
and creativity.
May you continue to share
the eccentricity
of your beautiful mind.

INTRODUCTION

The Throat Chakra

According to the Vedas (ancient Indian sacred texts), the physical body is composed of seven main energy or vortex centers called chakras. Chakra is the Sanskrit word for wheel.
The seven main chakras run along the spine-beginning from the root and ending with the crown chakra.

1. Root
2. Sacral
3. Solar plexus
4. Heart
5. Throat
6. Third eye
7. Crown

Each chakra has a different color, element, sound, mantra, function, location, major organ, and association. The flow or blockage/imbalance of subtle energy in each chakra determines the health or disease of the individual body.

This book is the third of a series of seven poetry books.

It is composed of poems associated with topics of the throat chakra. The throat chakra is the fifth chakra. It is the one associated with our expression, communication, voice, and truth.

Throat Chakra information:
Sanskrit name: Vishuddha
Color: Light blue, turquoise
Element: Sound
Sound: Ham
Mantra: "I Speak"
Practice: Mantra meditation
Function: Expression and communication
Location: Center of the neck
Organ: Throat, thyroid gland, vocal cords, jaw, mouth, teeth, cervical spine, shoulders, and arms
Associations: Expression of personal truth, honest speech, the power to create and follow one's dreams, sharing creative talents, verbal and nonverbal communication, practice of patience, and embracing silence and stillness
Dysfunctions when imbalanced: Sore throat, thyroid problems, tooth issues, stiff neck and shoulders, TMJ, addiction, being shy in expressing oneself, being gossipy, dishonest, withdrawn and unable to express through creativity.

1. ARTISTS INSPIRE ONE ANOTHER

Artists inspire
other artists to create.
The real purpose of creating something
is to share it
with your fellow man.
Let him judge and ridicule it
or rejoice in its beauty.
Artists relate to one another.
They speak a common
foreign language-
one whose whispers
echo loudly
and arise from the deepest place
of the collective Divine.

2. ARTIST'S EYES

How can you understand me?
No artist has ever been
nor will ever be
a puzzle easily revealed.
For only an artist
takes Truth for what it is-
sculpting reality
with a feathered pen
or elaborate instrument.
Perhaps,
a stained brush.
How can you imagine
the combination of color
reality provides
when you have never seen
through an artist's eyes?

3. ART

I've come to the conclusion
I will always be complete within
even if I lose everything.
This wholeness comes from knowing
I will forever have art
to please my heart.

4. PIECES EMBEDDED

Creative expression has a way
of touching us deeply.
I am grateful
for those courageous enough
to share pieces of themselves
with the rest of the world.
Pieces embedded
in music,
in poetry,
and in art
of any and all kind.

5. INSPIRATION FROM ABOVE

Solitary stillness is very underrated.
It is only in such instances
an artist is able to create.
Through these Divine moments
he receives inspiration from above.
This kind of inspiration
is the purest of all Love.
It shines Light on all it touches.

6. WE ARE ALL PHILOSOPHERS

We are all philosophers
for we function throughout our daily lives
in obedience to our own theories-
our personal beliefs.
How beautiful it is
to meet someone
who understands our work.

7. MISUNDERSTOOD

Being misunderstood by the majority
which lacks the capacity to understand
is not troubling at all.
It is when you are misunderstood by the minority
which has the capacity and chooses not to understand
that you shall find yourself troubled.

8. PEN AND PAPER

A pen and paper
will listen to you
at any hour of day or night.
Seeing clearly through the smoke-
reflections of the mind,
a mirror projecting your blurry image back to you-
giving you impeccable advice.
Pen and paper
are the greatest weapons in the world-
for a voice which has something
powerful to say
shall forever be heard.

9. AS ELUSIVE AS POETRY

Moments of love
are as elusive as poetry
which comes to you
when you have drunk too much.
Lacking the paper to inscribe
the powerful tide which takes you-
you are left bewildered
when you realize you never noticed
what happened,
what touched you in such an inexplicable way
and will never touch you
the same again.

10. NOTE TO SELF

And so,
I jot down a note to Self.
How many more will I be able to write
before the book runs out of pages?

11. SHORT DESCRIPTION

Philosopher's mind,
healer's hands,
lover's heart,
and child's smile!

12. POET

My heart is ink
and my mind is the pen
thus, I write
again and again!

13. THE POET

The best way to understand the poet
is to read his poetry,
for it is the voice
of his being.

14. POET DEFINED

Poet (noun): someone who uses the logical tool of words for the creative expression of emotions.

15. MOTHER OF POETRY

A poet deciding which poems are best
is like a mother choosing
which child she loves most.

16. THE POET'S WRATH

The poet's wrath
is never spoken of-
never whispered
by uncleansed mouths.
The poet's wrath
is sunk in silence,
sunk in pride
for it all lives inside.
The poet's wrath
is the poet's tool,
the poet's inspiration
to awaken the fool.
The poet's wrath
is present in his masterpiece-
present and inevitable,
in works which bring you peace.
The poet's wrath
is his own life,
his only way
to grow and strive.
If you wish to defeat it,
kill the poet herself.
For no poet ever lived
who never felt.

17. POETRY FOR THE AGES

We're all going to die.
Most of us die a bit daily of loneliness
and a feeling of never being understood
or seen for who we are.
In years to come,
nothing of us will exist the way it is now.
That's why poetry is so important.
It's a part of ourselves
we give the world
which will live on forever.
When future generations read it,
they may feel a bit less lonely,
as others once upon a time related to them.
We all share humanity
and the feelings which come along with being human.
Let's be kind to one another.

18. OLD POEMS

Looking back at old poems of mine,
it is apparent my writing has changed tremendously.
Which is a clear indication that I, as a person,
have as well.

Poetry is therapy.
Stay focused on the path-
faithful like Penelope.

20. BLANK PAGES

No matter what comes your way,
turn to blank pages
and fill them with life-
stories locked within the cage of your mind.
No matter what painful situations
make the heart die,
resurrection lays
on a naked page
awaiting your expression.
So, when times are lovely
or when they're too much to bear,
know that poetry
will be there.

21. THE WORD

Why use the fist
when the tongue is stronger?
The tongue is the most
powerful weapon in the world
for it is the vessel of Truth
and Truth is spoken through it.

22. WORD IS BOND

Word is bond.

We sign contracts when we
talk with one another.
Let's speak wisdom
into each other.

We cast spells
in our writing.
A seeker of Truth
abstains from lying.

Let the voice be
your greatest weapon.
Use it to empower
and connect as one.

23. WORDS AS BRICKS

Words build on words
as bricks on bricks.
You create a sentence,
a paragraph,
a book,
a tower of information so high-
built with discipline and dedication.
Creations starting from
something so tiny,
but the tool was your mind.

24. A WRITING

Life is a writing.
When you first pick up a pen
and place it on the paper,
you don't know what will come out of it
or where it will lead.
But as the hand moves,
everything falls into place
and ends up making sense.
Life is a story written by us-
the best storytellers.
So, we must keep writing
until the ink and paper are used up
for without one the other can still function.
A pen may write on flesh
and to substitute ink
we may use blood.

25. SPIRIT OF WRITING

When you write-
all inhibitions are lost.
It's just you and the paper.
And to this bond
you can be more honest
than even with yourself.

26. WRITING IS MEDITATION

Writing is therapeutic.
It is a friend who helps you understand all sides of yourself
and all of your different voices.
Writing shows you who you are because it is a part of you.
It is therapeutic because it is meditation.
Meditation is a delving into your being-
being kind with and accepting of all you find there,
especially the parts you're ashamed of!
It's okay to be ashamed of your human flaws.
Only by accepting them can you begin
to change them and to evolve.

27. WE LEARN

When we talk with other human beings
we listen to a new perspective
from others who have had different experiences than us.
We learn.
Reading is valuable for this reason.
Through reading,
we obtain another perspective
from someone who sees the world in a new way.
The author teaches us other methods of thinking.
Whichever touch us,
we can incorporate into our own lives.

28. STORY OF OUR LIVES

It's a long, painful
and complicated story-
this story of our lives.

Beautiful and Abundant Universe,
please grant me the strength to endure
all trials and tribulations which come my way.
Provide me with humor so I may smile
even during the darkest moments of my life.
Fill me with gratitude for the time
I am present here on Earth.
Pour all of your Light within my broken spaces
so I may live on in honor of you each passing day.
Guide me towards humility
so I may share all of you with every being which crosses my path.
Most of all,
give me courage to love fearlessly.
Courage to seek and exist only in Truth.
Allow me to be the physical embodiment
and vessel of that which is Godly.
Bless my tongue with words of wisdom.
Show me the journey towards you.
Lift my spirit high enough
so I may surpass all human shortcomings.
I am an expression of you in this realm.
Only to humbly return to you again one day.

30. TATTOOED CORPSE

How do you think this one died?
Perhaps, it was a cancer which grew
and fiercely spread throughout the body
as evil does overlooking human will.
Or maybe, it was a slower beat of the heart
which caused him to feel chest pains
and rush to the hospital, but inevitably
enter its doors too late.
The emergency gave way.
Hold the bed for another
tired soul or better yet,
another day.

How do you think this one died?
He looks fairly old and satisfied.
Maybe it was time's calling which carried
this corpse away.
He does look ancient
with his hairless head tilted to the side,
but then again, younger men
have lost it all too soon.
But the wrinkles don't lie
as they shape parallel lines
on the forehead and edges of the mouth.
He must have been an enthusiastic spirit,
one which laughed much and bedded
many seductively, innocent mistresses.

How do you think this one died?
Perhaps, he got stabbed
as he defended his pal
during a bar brawl.
He looks like he was rather frisky,
easily excitable, and given way to emotion.
It was possibly during a drunken state
he went into the parlor
and told the artist to draw
onto his right arm
a design which would whisper it all.
But that was when his breath could flow
exhale and inhale with ease.
Now the youngster is gone
and resting in peace
while only soul and tattoo carry on.

31. PARADOXES

Paradoxes are astonishing.
They say so much,
yet make little sense all at once.
Oxymorons are the same
as they unwrap meaning
through contradiction.
Opposite extremes combine.
They open up the mind,
they bring new awareness
and Truth-
ideas of youth.
To avoid the extremes is perfection;
to combine them is genius!

32. URGENCY

The urgency with which we live
is the urgency with which we write.
For it is the writers' yearning to share
their adventures and experience.
To be enclosed in a dark room
with pen and paper
is of no use.
Show me a person who has explored the world
and I shall call him a poet,
a lover.
Poetry and love are one.
Both exist to be shared with the world.

33. CREATE

Here I find
another blank page
on which to write.
Another empty space
on which to build.
This is my destiny revealed.

I create.

Here I see
another open wound
and pain is what I feel.
It is time for me to heal.

I create.

Life-
with every inhalation
and every smile I share
in loving expression.
Art-
with every color, word, embrace.
I create beauty's face.

34. AN ARTIST'S TOOL

The stage is prepared,
the lights are all set,
the audio repaired
and the timing is met.

Actors enter proudly
to recite their lines-
with lighting so bright
their character shines.

The role in act
is the truth within.
Swapping lies with fact,
frown and grin.

Reality is sketched
to blend on the stage.
Emotion is stretched
to fit on the page.

35. ACTORS

The greatest actors become consumed
in their character roles.
It becomes hard to distinguish
between them and their soul.
The greatest actors are free
and simultaneously slaves.
Reality is a blur
as becomes the stage.

36. WORDS AWAITING SOUND

As the words flow through
and onto this page,
I imagine someone playing
an instrument with rage.
And I see it clearly now
this reading he must avow.

As the words pour out,
it's all about the beat
and someone's playing a tune
with lyrics he has yet to meet.
And I see it clearly now
his spirit's leading mine somehow.

As the words come freely
and he oh so dearly jams,
this song's causing us to be
each other's biggest fans.
And I see it clearly now
this calling I must avow.

As the words clear the mess
of the mind's scattered pile,
the lyrics to his songs
have been written all the while.
And I see it clearly now
this bond we must avow.

37. PHOTOGRAPHS

Time may escape us
and our passions may subside,
but photographs capture eternity
for in them it resides.

You take an image
clearly seen before you-
one which is temporary,
simple and natural-
simply natural.

You look through your lens
and you construct
forms completely unknown
to anyone or anything
but your own mind-
forms which become permanently
engraved in the heart.

This is the artist's way.
Let the spirit take its toll
and beauty thus control.

The Universe influences artists
and, in turn,
artists create new universes.

Each creation is

a mountain of feelings,
a field of thoughts.
Each person looking
through the lens
interprets the reality
of these illusions
in his unique way.

This is the artist's way.
Let the spirit take its toll
and beauty thus control.
The time may escape us
and our passions may subside,
but photographs capture eternity
for in them it resides.

38. CAPTURE MOMENTS

Memory may fail us-
many times it does,
but photographs capture moments
of what once was.

Experience may be vague
in the body's scattered mind,
but photographs capture memories
long left behind.

The camera may be hidden
and difficult to use,
but photographs capture moments
which pleasant memories seduce.

39. STORY ON THE JOURNEY

Pictures capture youth and innocence-
not yet beaten down by life experience,
yet not as wise as now.
We capture moments in time
and revisit them along the way.
We get to see our story as it is unfolding
from our first day
until our very last.
Everything tells a fragment of the story-
from the wrinkles on our face
to the strength we build in our body
and the subtle voice of intuition and guidance
which we eventually learn to trust.
Capturing our story on
the journey to Source.

40. THE GREATEST

The greatest of men
and wo-men
are those who have understood themselves,
cultivated themselves,
and fearlessly shared their talents with the world.

41. SHARE

I have come to find
it is our responsibility
to share our passion and talent with the world.

42. FOR ALL THE MIND HAS RENDERED

What great pleasure it would give
to see my name written
with exclusion of red corrections.

To bear it written on blank paper,
merely blending with the rest.

What great pleasure it would give
to see my name written
with exclusion of attention.

To bear it written on paper blank,
shown as a sign of greatness.

What great pleasure it would give
to see my name written
so plain as it is,

alongside wise men
for decades now remembered.

Such pleasure would help me
rejoice in humbleness
for all the mind has rendered.

43. TALENTED

We may be naturally talented at something,
yet never even be aware of it-
unless, of course, we choose to expand our narrow horizons
and try new things.

44. MUSIC WITHOUT LYRICS

Music without lyrics-
a blank canvas on which to paint,
an empty book to fill with your own writings.

45. MUSIC TAKE CONTROL

If ever you feel down
turn it all around!
Twist the body so-
let the music take control.

46. MUSIC IS UNIVERSAL

Music is universal and speaks to all souls.
Therefore, it is a friend of mine.

47. MUSIC TUNES

Isn't it incredible
how music will follow you
wherever you go?
It sails with you across the oceans,
up the high and down the low.
You hear the same tune in a different nation
and another state of mind.
Yet, it touches you the same
wherever your soul it'll find.

48. THE WILD'S MUSIC

Nature is creating music.
The water is singing
and the wind is playing saxophone.
The leaves are dancing
to the tune alone.
The bridge is standing still
in midst of all of this
and the couple under it
is sharing their first kiss.

49. GIFT OF MUSIC

Whoever left,
left behind
the gift of music.
For this I am grateful.

50. I HAVE MUSIC

Everyone has love,
but I have music.
I have words-
words I can turn into lyrics
any time I wish.
But all you have is an elusive kiss.

51. MUSIC IS MY ONLY HOPE

It's cold outside
so, I need some music
to warm me up
and keep my heart
in place.
Better than just any
false embrace.
People drain in their own way.
I need art to keep me sane
and allow me to be
myself today.
So, music is
my only hope.
If it were a man,
I would already have eloped.

52. THE CORDS

Musical cords exist as are
when not meddled with.
Some say they're beautiful
in this stationary state.
But if artists believed the same
there would be no music.
So don't tell me things are perfect
just the way they are.
Don't say they should never change.
Don't deprive us
of your music.

53. SAXOPHONE BEAT

The sound.
We can all hear it.
We embrace it with our movement.
From a distance it is present
in our minds,
our ears.
Saxophone beats.
The man who remains
in the cold to warm our hearts.
The New York City lights,
the smell,
the taste of the city air,
the traffic commotion,
the horse manure;
the pride in such animals.
The fast pace of rush hour.
The sound still following us.
The sound.
If everything else is different
the sound is all we share
on this brisk evening.
All of us, strangers, which pass each other,
walking to our separate worlds.
The saxophone.
Becoming strong with every step,
every beat.
It will remain in my mind
as the most peaceful moment.

Harmoniously walking toward my future.
The saxophone!
The bond which connects all human souls.

Dedicated to the stranger with the talent to play so well.
You enriched my night with your sound.
Thank you!

54. SWEETEST RHYMES

It does thus indicate
the passing of the times-
for who has ever lived a beat
without his sweetest rhymes?
And my dear fellow soul
which feels the energies about-
tell me what life would be
in presence without.

55. RECORDINGS

When we record ourselves in audio or visual,
we are able to capture our progression.
It's an observer's diary
and that is incredible.
We get to grow old with ourselves.

56. SOUND

Have you heard
the movement of the wind
as it dances in the night
so smoothly
flowing past the stars and the trees?
Have you heard
the mating call of birds
and the sweet love songs
they chirp in early morning?
Have you heard
the beating of your heart
as blood pumps
in and out
constantly keeping you alive?
Oh, what it means to embrace
the silence and stillness
of an unquiet mind!
Have you heard
any true sound
beyond the noise
of your thoughts?

57. LOUDER

Sometimes,
you will interact with someone
who values your mind
in the deepest ways.
A person who listens to your thoughts
and shows you how
differently beautiful your perspective is.
This person will see
your intuitive nature
and admire you for it.
So, you come to realize
you really are special.
Even if you were too humble
to admit this before.
Even if previously you assumed
everyone loves like you
and lives with your depth.
You see a person who is a mirror
reflecting the eternal beauty
of your mind and soul.
And this "seeing" of you
will be your creative vessel.
A voice which has something to say
can never be silenced,
but it can be inspired to speak
just a little bit louder.

58. BLANK SLATE

Look at the painting
with all those crazy colors.
And to think,
it was once a blank slate!

59. UNEASINESS

Sleepless nights filled with thoughts
about life, longings, dreams, ambitions.
Silences disrupted with endless chatter of the mind.
A place of home to every writer, lover, great thinker.
Embrace your battle.
Uneasiness is a sign you're alive.

60. STAND STILL

We are at a crossroads, you and I.
We only meet when we stand still.

61. SILENCE AND STILLNESS

Use the silence and stillness in your presence
to speak to others with love and light.

62. HIS GREATEST CREATION

Ironically enough,
there comes a time when the poet has nothing left to say,
words would only burden the heart,
and silence is his greatest creation.

63. STILLING THE MIND

Stilling the mind is a daily practice-
a worthy journey through the darkness of the mind.
Only after traveling through the abyss
do we learn to ease it into stillness.
Befriending our shadow side helps us to keep it in check.
We must be resilient in the process.
Otherwise, it will swallow us whole.
So, if you find yourself in the dark, continue pushing forward.
I'll see you all on the other, brighter side!

64. TRULY STILL

No living creature is ever truly still-
though he may appear to be.

65. ART OF MEDITATION

We call it the art of meditation
because meditation is an art
and through art we meditate.

We cannot discuss art without discussing the art of meditation.
The very act of creation-
creativity is Divine inspiration.
It is in those creative and meditative moments of flow
where the artist is the vessel for the Ultimate Creator
to express Himself.

66. CREATOR

Nothing compares to the feeling
which comes in creating.
It's a unique kind of joy.
It's the closest we commune with our Creator,
our Source,
our God.
It's meditation.
It's our very nature.
To connect with our true Self
through creativity
as a vessel
is simply breathtaking.
It's awe inspiring
to look up at the quiet and solitary
existence we come from.
It is in those still spaces of our lives
we truly understand
who we are and what we are here for.
We see then
we are no different-
we're a union of spirits
in Divine moments
of eternal connection.
Thus, I am happy
to share of myself
through my words
and my actions
with the rest of you.

67. SPEECHLESS

Only the best and worst of times
leave a poet speechless.

68. UNNOTICED

Maybe if I stay quiet enough
I will go unnoticed-
like an echo
lost in the wind and unheard
or self-inflicted bruises long forgotten.
Maybe I will go unnoticed
or maybe, just maybe,
I will be understood.

69. QUIET ROOM

Life is a quiet room.
You only hear what your mind tells you.
Internal chatter with small intervals of absolute silence.
A silence so clearly stating
how temporary these walls are.
Walls of brick, wood,
flesh and bone.
All to be torn
down one day
and brought to dust.
We are dissipating corpses which contain Consciousness.
So I cry.
I sit and I weep.
Not out of fear.
I cry because of the awareness of life's true essence.
Nothing really matters.
There's nothing to hold on to
and in its truest meaning,
each of us is alone
within the Collective.

70. SPOKEN WORDS

Words can never express
all the love and tenderness
I learned to experience
inside of your embrace.
Words can never be found
to ever amount
to the paramount
challenges we face.
Words are just sounds
which echo about,
which scream very loud
of momentary beauty.
Words are cruel and cold,
can never shape or mold
the hearts which grow tired and old,
but only love see.

71. NEVER SPEAK WORDS

Never speak words
which don't come from the heart
for you will be the victim
of your lies from the start.
Never speak words
without feeling them first.
Never shower another
to defeat your thirst.
Never speak words
or lies which are foul
for others will remember
all to the vowel.

72. SPEAK THE TRUTH YOU ARE SEEING

Who am I
and what is this "I"
each of us recalls?
Is it the name we have been given?
The masks we use to play our roles?
The family which brought us here;
maybe it knows.
Is it the skin we're doomed to wear?
The hidden smile
or lonely stare?
Is it the lips of red
and almond-shaped eyes?
Or the drifting thoughts within the head
and wisdom which within resides?
Tell me my fellow being.
Give me something to define.
Speak the truth you are seeing
and I shall tell you mine!

73. SPEAKING WITH NATURE

The times when
the only sound I hear
is the wind's echo on the leaves,
the distant singing of the birds,
the poetry of the silent sky.
These are the times
when I feel most alive.
How can anyone feel alone here?
Be present and grounded
when speaking with nature.

74. LISTEN TO ME

Once you tell people your situation
they will give their opinions
and their solutions
even if all you wanted was a listening
and empathic presence.
One of the areas humanity fails horribly in
is listening!

I don't mean hearing-
that we've been trained to do
as if we were robots.
We can hear numerous facts
all at once.
But what are we really gaining?
Certainly not knowledge
if we aren't listening.

And if we aren't listening
we aren't truly caring either
because if we aim to understand another
we must listen to him when he speaks.
For the tongue
is his sharpest tool
and it guides us to his
heart, soul, and mind.

75. UNAPOLOGETICALLY

I am not afraid to express who I am.
I am Truth and Love personified.
I will always carry the strength
to be honest, humble, and caring.
I will not be scared
of other's judgements and ridicule.
I will not fear other's disapproval
or intimidation of my power.
I will continue to be me,
unapologetically and bravely.

As I sit here
in twilight's hour
I prepare the tongue
to spit some fire.
And so it goes
in lonely times,
poets find solace
within their rhymes.
As sorrow creeps in
through the window,
thus, isolation's knife
kills extra slow.
And so,
as I sit here
all alone
it's clear-
solitude is all we've ever known.
This poem is for the sensitive ones
who befriended despair
like new born infants
breathing in the air.
I know too well
what it's like
to live in the shadows
all your life.
With so much love
and wisdom to share
into a nothingness

that's always there.
So, as I sit here
in twilight's hour
I sharpen my tongue
to spit some fire.
Let it burn,
turn me to dust.
Let my death speak volumes
if it must.

77. DEFENSE

Poetry is my only form of expression,
my only salvation,
the only defense I have
against the dangerous mind.

78. EXISTS IN ITSELF

Truth exists in itself.
It exists regardless of who agrees or disagrees with it.
It blossoms even if others are afraid of it.
It thrives even if you feel uncomfortable by it.
Truth doesn't need to defend itself.
It remains present awaiting your courage and awareness.

79. CLOSER

People fear silence because it brings them closer together.

80. THE GIFT OF HONESTY

The best gift you can give a person you love is your honesty.
You respect someone when you tell him the truth.
You respect his presence
and trust in his strength and ability
to overcome painful realities.
It also shows you are brave enough to own up to yourself.
It is the ultimate expression of love
for thyself and for another being.

81. SPEAK FOR ITSELF

No words can describe
or do justice to us,
so I'll let this love
speak for itself.

82. THE HARD TRUTH

The hard truth is
one day you will separate
from every person you love,
even if you live your life together.
Death is a silent goodbye
or at the very least
a "see you later."
Either they will leave first
or you will.
So what the fuck is there
to hold on to?

83. TRUTH HURTS

Truth lays beyond that which we wish to believe,
choose to believe,
think we believe.
It has a secret identity
and sometimes it inevitably hurts tremendously.

84. FALSEHOODS

All falsehoods only exist
when we are alive.

85. SARCASTIC ONE

There are two interpretations
of thoughts inside my head.
You are the dark, sarcastic one.

86. HIGH

Today I reached up high,
reached up to grab
the intelligent mind-
the universal mind
which will never confine
the spirit's desire to grow.

87. IMMEDIATE EXPRESSION

Words.
They are the immediate expression of thought–
they come and they go,
impermanent like all which exists.
They alter and adapt
like flickering butterfly wings
or sand washed away
from the shore,
drawn into the depths of the ocean.

88. ECHOED

Nothing I will ever say is new.
I know this to be true.
I'm merely hoping words which have been
previously echoed
touch old souls in a new way.

89. DISTORTED SOUNDS

The sounds which scream to be heard
and voices which struggle to be understood.

90. COLLECTIVE UNCONSCIOUS

Anything I ever had to say
has been told ages before me.
Maybe in a different language,
in a different period,
a comma added in another state.
Nonetheless,
its voice has been echoed
long before me
in the Collective Unconscious.

91. APPRECIATE GREAT MINDS

I was put on this Earth to create and when I don't,
everything around me seems to rapidly shut down.
Present times hardly appreciate or acknowledge
creative minds.
But maybe,
just maybe,
I am here to change this.

Met another one
yet again.
Keep coming into close contact
with them
as if they were flies
which constantly creep up
on top of my kitchen table
searching for something,
anything on which to feed.
Damn flies
which attack in packs.
Met another one
yet again.
Saw the ruthless passion
in their bloodshot eyes-
that of parasites
which destroy and live off
everything around them.
Lousy artists.

93. MEETINGS

Meeting individuals with great depth
is a rare occurrence.
Most of the ones I have met are currently dead
in bodily form.
But their spirit surely lives
for it is through their writings
we have become acquainted.

94. OUR SENSITIVITY

Our introversion and our sensitivity is our beauty.
It's our intuition-
our spirituality and our knowing,
the childlike spirit which lives on always,
alive within us.

95. DEGREE

In too long or short a time-
all which differs is the degree of impatience.

96. LIFE

There's another train coming soon.
Just be patient and it will be here
before you know it.

97. ON THE 1 TRAIN

I took the 1 train
to 111 Street
on the 11th day of the month
and my train car number was 11.
On the train,
the conductor announced service was suspended-
there was a fire on another station's tracks.
Most people of the packed train stormed out
in panic and agitation.
I decided to stay on and wait it out.
In moments like these we get to practice
and build up our patience muscles.
Quickly afterwards, the conductor said
"The next stop is..."
and just like that
we took off.
I think about those who left the train.
How they must've been in anger and stress
trying to find another way to their destination.
If only we just relax and remain patient
then we can ride the nearly empty train
while sitting down and going where we need to go sooner.
This subway car is a metaphor for life itself.

98. TRUST

Trust is the only concept every person views the same.
Regardless of what you believe in,
trust is the one word which means the same
to me, you, and everyone else.

99. ELUSIVE MEANING

Sometimes,
I long for deep conversation
about the elusive meaning
life's shade provides.
The elusive meaning it has for you.
As I share my purpose
and my passions
with anyone willing to listen
to an old and tired soul.
Sometimes,
I long to let
this trembling and hoarse voice
echo visions of carefree moments
held onto only in a flash of light-
moments as elusive as
the meaning of life.

100. TRUTH OF LIFE

There are times I ponder
about the purpose of life.
The positive optimists would say it is to be happy,
to do those things which satisfy the heart.
The pessimists would say life is hard
and finding what truly makes us happy is difficult.
But someone who looks at existence
from the lens of the observer
(the neutral, rational realist)
would say there is no purpose at all
beyond that which we choose.
Moments of both-
happiness and sadness-
are inevitable.
All moments are temporary and fleeting-
however beautiful or cruel they may be.
So, I conclude all we can do in life is simply be.
This is not to be understood
as a positive or negative statement.
Simply as a Truth of life.

101. UNDERSTAND

The way an empath thinks and lives
is something very rare.
For this reason
few can truly understand him,
but he understands everyone.
I doubt there is
a lonelier existence than this.

102. TO SOURCE I SAY

Lift the clouds from my eyes
so I may see the way.
Lift the sorrow from my heart
so I may shine my light.
Lift the grief from my mind
so I may smile today.
Lift the loneliness from my being
so I may sleep tonight.

103. AFFIRMATION

I remove all the negative from within myself
and only keep the light.
I remove all which is hurtful and painful
for it is not who I truly am.
I remove all within me which does not help me grow.

I am grounded.
I feel the Earth
beneath my hands and feet.
I am water as my hips flow.
I am sensual desire
and wildfire.
I am love and letting go.
I am sound,
the voice of Truth.
I am vision and I see.
I am Divinity.

105. SWEET UNIVERSE

Oh, sweet and dearest Universe-
use me as your vessel,
manipulate me as your tool
to spread and emanate
your brightest Light.
Shine through into the darkness
which resides in hearts and beings.
Use me as your voice
and your pen
to express words of Truth
and everlasting Love
in a constantly changing flux of existence.
Oh, sweetest of sweet life-
let me be a guide into the Eternal.

I choose compassion.
I choose love.
I choose forgiveness.
I choose to embody my Highest Self.
I choose to embrace my Abundance.
I choose to live a life of peace and joy.
I choose to let go of past hurts.
I choose to be present in the beautiful Now.
I choose the path of greatest purpose and service to the world.
I choose humbleness.
I choose creativity.
I choose connection to Source.
Tonight on this full moon and every moment of my life.
And so it is,
and so it is,
and so it is.

107. COMPASSIONATE COMMUNICATION

Compassionate communication
should exist in all our relationships-
with romantic partners,
friends,
family members,
and ourselves.
Expressing our voice and embodying our truth
creates an open and healthy environment in relationship.
Relating through honesty helps us grow
(together and individually as well).
Courageously living in our truth isn't always easy,
but it is necessary.

108. COMMUNICATION

Communication's been cut off
and now you're working on machines.
You're breathing slowly on them
as they monitor your dreams.

Your senses have been shattered
and you now seem so weak.
The machine is operating well.
Your heart has reached its peak!

You must be very cautious though
for soon it might explode
from all the damaging effects
of years it has endured.

109. COMPLAINING IS USELESS

Complaining is useless.
If you don't like something about your life
then change it.
If you can't change it,
sit back and practice patience
until it changes on its own.
Or, perhaps, you are the one who will change.
Change is the only constant.

When you make the conscious decision
to avoid complaining,
you become aware of how often
you have been doing so.
You also become aware of how often
others do so every day.

Most interaction
and human exchange is full of this
negative, low vibrational energy.
I wonder how it became the norm in such a way.

A bit of awareness helps us improve and elevate.
Through awareness we see the truth of what is.
Therefore, we are able to alter the things which
don't serve our Higher Self.

Life is too amazing to be lived in such a stagnant place.
We are here briefly.
Use the opportunity of presence
to experience and create through Love.
Tap into your inner power;
the power of manifestation and magic.
Embrace abundance.

iii. LEFT TO SAY

I haven't written in a while.
I guess there's not much left to say.

-ACKNOWLEDGMENTS-

I am grateful to everyone who made this book possible.

Thank you to my editor, Jaclyn Reuter.
Thank you to my formatter, Nola Li Barr.
Thank you to my cover designer, Danijela Mijailovic.

Thank you to my amazing family-Galatia Kitsios, Spiro Kitsios, and Ioannis Kitsios. Your ongoing support and love has sculpted me into the person I am today. Family is the most valuable part of the human experience and I am eternally grateful to be a member of ours.

Thank you to all of my friends, clients, and colleagues. Everyone is my teacher as I learn something new every single day.

Thank you to my Coffee Ave family for creating such a homey, cozy, and friendly space where I organized and completed this series of books. Your café has helped me focus and manifest my dream. I am especially grateful to Neo, Beldry, and Dimitri for their kindness and friendship.

My gratitude goes out to everyone who has been a part of my healing journey and this incredible opportunity (life) for spiritual evolution.

May we rejoice in presence and silence with each other.
May we continue to speak power and love into one another.
Namaste.

~ABOUT THE AUTHOR~

Maria Kitsios is a New York licensed massage therapist and a Reiki master since 2013. Before dedicating her life to these healing modalities, she obtained a bachelor's degree in Behavioral Science. In September of 2021, she became a certified yoga instructor and published her first book, *The Journey to Source*. *The Journey to Source* is composed of poems associated with the crown chakra and is the first of the series of seven books. Shortly after, she published her second book of the series, *Unravel the Veil*. *Unravel the Veil* is composed of poems associated with the third eye chakra. This book is the third of the same series.

Join Maria's newsletter
and receive a free copy of the asanas guideline.

www.subscribepage.com/thejourneytosourceasanas

Instagram: @mkitsioslmt
Facebook: @Maria Kitsios, LMT

66261738R00129